Date: 2/1/12

First Facts®

Snakes

Boa Constrictors

by Joanne Mattern

Consultant:
Robert T. Mason, PhD
Professor of Zoology
J.C. Braly Curator of Vertebrates
Oregon State University, Corvallis

Capstone
press®

Mankato, Minnesota

First Facts is published by Capstone Press,
151 Good Counsel Drive, P.O. Box 669, Mankato, Minnesota 56002.
www.capstonepress.com

Library of Congress Cataloging-in-Publication Data
Mattern, Joanne, 1963–
   Boa constrictors / by Joanne Mattern.
   p. cm. — (First facts. Snakes)
   Includes bibliographical references and index.
   Summary: "A brief introduction to boa constrictors, including their habitat, food,
and life cycle" — Provided by publisher.
   ISBN-13: 978-1-4296-1922-6 (hardcover)
   ISBN-10: 1-4296-1922-8 (hardcover)
   1. Boa constrictor — Juvenile literature. I. Title.
QL666.O63M369 2009
597.96'7 — dc22
                                         2007051890

Editorial Credits

Lori Shores, editor; Ted Williams, designer and illustrator; Danielle Ceminsky,
   illustrator; Jo Miller, photo researcher

Photo Credits

Dreamstime/Woutervanderwiel, 20
Getty Images Inc./Minden Pictures/Claus Meyer, cover; Michael & Patricia Fogden, 8;
   Peter Oxford, 11
McDonald Wildlife Photography/Joe McDonald, 5, 12–13
Pete Carmichael, 17
Peter Arnold/J. Kobel, 7
Photo Researchers Inc/Toni Angermayer, 19
Shutterstock/Chelmodeev Alexander Vasilyevich, 21; Dr. Morley Read, 14; Eric Isselee,
   1, 6; Nahimoff, background texture (throughout)
Visuals Unlimited/Jim Merli, 16

Essential content terms are **bold** and are defined at the bottom of the page where they first appear.

012010
5652VMI

Table of Contents

Meet the Boa Constrictor

You wouldn't want a hug from this big snake! Boa constrictors don't actually hug. Instead, boas use their big, powerful bodies to squeeze other animals to death. Boas squeeze so hard the animals can't breathe.

Boa constrictors are 6 to 10 feet (1.8 to 3 meters) long. They are about as long as a car. These snakes can weigh more than 60 pounds (27 kilograms).

Fun Fact!
Unlike people, boa constrictors keep growing all through their lives.

A Boa's Body

Boa constrictors are covered with scales. All snakes have these small pieces of hard skin. Snakes shed their scaly skin as they grow.

All snakes are **cold-blooded** reptiles.
Their bodies are the same temperature
as the air and ground around them.
Boas lie in the sun to warm their bodies.

Colors and Camouflage

It's hard to see a boa constrictor lying on the ground. That's because the snake's patterns and colors provide great **camouflage**. Boa constrictors' bodies are covered with patterns of ovals and diamonds. Boas can be brown, tan, gray, and black.

Fun Fact!
The boa constrictor's coloring is lightest at its head and darkest down by its tail.

A Hot, Wet Home

Boa constrictors are right at home in hot, wet areas. They are found in Central America and South America. Most boas live in the rain forest.

Boa Constrictor Range

☐ where boa constrictors live

North America

Europe

Asia

Africa

South America

Australia

Antarctica

The rain forest is warm all year long. That means boa constrictors are active all year. They do not **hibernate** like snakes in cooler areas.

hibernate: to spend winter in a resting state as if in a deep sleep

The Big Squeeze

Boa constrictors get their name because they **constrict** other animals. A boa wraps its strong body around the unlucky **prey**. The boa squeezes tighter and tighter until the animal stops breathing.

Fun Fact!
Boa constrictors eat birds, rats, bats, and lizards. They even eat monkeys.

constrict: to squeeze tightly
prey: an animal hunted for food

tongue

heat sensors

Super Senses

Boa constrictors have special heat sensors along the edge of their mouths. These organs can sense warm-blooded animals that come near.

Snakes also use their sense of smell to find prey. But they can smell with more than just their noses. Boas use their forked tongues to pick up scents from the air. A special organ in the snake's mouth identifies the smells.

Open Wide!

A boa constrictor can swallow animals larger than its mouth. Its jaw is not joined like a human jaw. Snake jaws are stretchy and can open very wide.

A boa grabs prey with its mouth. But dinner isn't served yet. The snake still has hard work to do. Powerful muscles move the prey into its stomach.

Fun Fact!

It takes some time for a boa to digest a whole animal. The snake might not eat again for many days or weeks.

17

Growing Up

Male and female boas mate in the spring. The female carries babies inside her body. The babies develop for three to five months. In summer, a **brood** of baby snakes is born.

Mother boas leave after giving birth. The young snakes take care of themselves right away. Young boas can hunt mice and baby birds right away.

Fun Fact!

Unlike some other snakes, the boa constrictor does not lay eggs. Boas give birth to live babies.

brood: a group of snakes born at the same time

Life Cycle of a Boa Constrictor

Newborn
About 20 to 60 snakes are born at once.

Young
Young boas can triple their size in the first year.

Adult
Boa constrictors are ready to mate in three to four years.

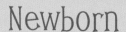

Brood

19

Living Long and Large

Some lizards and birds eat baby boas. But few animals dare to come near an adult boa constrictor. In the wild, boas can live as long as 30 years.

Amazing but True!

People all over the world keep boa constrictors as pets. They are usually kept in large cages. But in parts of South America, pet boas don't live in cages. They live in and around the house. These pet boas catch rats and other pests.

Glossary

brood (BROOHD) — a group of young animals born at the same time

camouflage (KAM-uh-flahzh) — coloring that makes animals, people, and objects look like their surroundings

cold-blooded (KOHLD-BLUH-id) — having a body temperature that changes with surroundings

constrict (kuhn-STRIKT) — to squeeze tightly to limit or prevent breathing

hibernate (HYE-bur-nate) — to spend winter in a resting state as if in a deep sleep

prey (PRAY) — an animal hunted by another animal for food

Read More

Bredeson, Carmen. *Boa Constrictors Up Close.* Zoom in on Animals. Berkeley Heights, N.J.: Enslow Elementary, 2006.

Doeden, Matt. *Boa Constrictors.* World of Reptiles. Mankato, Minn.: Capstone Press, 2005.

O'Hare, Ted. *Boas.* Amazing Snakes. Vero Beach, Fla.: Rourke, 2005.

Internet Sites

FactHound offers a safe, fun way to find Internet sites related to this book. All of the sites on FactHound have been researched by our staff.

Here's how:
1. Visit *www.facthound.com*
2. Choose your grade level.
3. Type in this book ID **1429619228** for age-appropriate sites. You may also browse subjects by clicking on letters, or by clicking on pictures and words.
4. Click on the **Fetch It** button.

FactHound will fetch the best sites for you!

Index